DUSTY *Crowns*

Dusting Yourselves off from the Inside Out

Eliminating the distractions and becoming the
woman God called you to be.

Heather Lindsey

Dedication

This book is dedicated to my best friend, Delan Broadway. When I first started to write this book, she encouraged me to say the unpopular and write what the Lord placed on my heart. She has stood by me since 2000 and I am thankful for her amazing friendship. Best, thank you for your boldness, encouragement and simply always being there for me. In season and out of season, you have been there, consistent and true. I love you forever.

My Prayer

Father, in the name of Jesus, I pray that you use this book to wreck these women from the inside out. Encourage them to let go of any distractions, hurts or pains and to read this book with an open heart. We rebuke any satanic or demonic attacks and I pray that these ladies strive to be bold and courageous in obeying You, Lord! In Jesus name, Amen!

I pray God uses this book to dig into your heart sister. I pray He shines the light on your heart and that He reveals the dark places. I pray you learn to trust Him and you allow for your identity to be found in Him alone and nothing else.

Acknowledgments

Thank you to my Lord and Savior, Jesus Christ. I simply could not even think, breathe or live without you. I do not take today or anything you have done in my life or heart for granted. Thank you for choosing me to write this book and share what you have shared with me. I look forward to the day when I see you face to face.

To my husband, Cornelius Lindsey: Thank you for inspiring me to write yet another book. You constantly push me towards Jesus and I am thankful for your love, your leadership and your heart. You challenge me to be better and to feed on the true meat of the word of God. (Since I will never eat physical meat! ☺) I love you babe. You are my cuppycake, my sweetheart, my love, my heart.

To my Logan: My son, you motivate me to be a better Christian, mommy, wife, friend and person. You inspired so much of this book because I have learned so much from being your mama. Thank you for your joy. Thank you for your heart. Thank you for being our son. I will seriously love and support you forever.

To my mama, Linda Canter: Thank you for encouraging me and always supporting me. I love you so much and I appreciate your love and encouragement.

To my birth mama, Kathleen Marcotulli: Thank you for giving me a chance at life. You gave me my start and I am thankful God has connected us back together again. I love you!

To my family: Words cannot express how much I love and appreciate ya'll! You've embraced what the Lord has called me to do and you step in and help wherever's needed. Thank you for your willingness. You're so loved.

To my birth family: You all are so supportive and encouraging! I've only known you for a short period of time, but you all welcomed me with open arms and truly made me feel like family. Thank you. I love you all!

To my Pinky Promise Sisters: Thanks for always supporting me and loving on me! I am thankful to be a part of the most amazing organization ever!

Table of Contents

CHAPTER 1

Where is My Heart?

I once hated myself. I hated everything about myself. I hated my forehead, my nose, my hair, my skin, my body and I made it a second job to tear my image apart. Have you ever done this? For years in my life, I spent more time ripping myself apart rather than accepting myself the way God made me—for His purpose and glory. My heart was so ugly because I was jealous of others, I was insecure about my life and I did not believe God had a plan for me. Have you ever felt this way? What about you? If you were to take a mirror and shine it on your heart—what would it expose? What would your heart say? Are you constantly running to God and asking Him for His "blessings", "favor" and breakthrough, but then totally ignoring the sin that you are living in?

Maybe, like me, you beat yourself up physically. Maybe you are living with your man. Or maybe, you are living apart, but stay the night together every night. Maybe you are married, but you are totally rebellious in your heart. Maybe, you are married but your mind is constantly with an ex-boyfriend. Maybe you are just plain mean. Maybe you lie about everything. Maybe you hate everyone and everything. Maybe you like to curse. Maybe you like to get drunk. Maybe you like to have sex outside of marriage. If this is the case, honey, the only breakthrough you need is to REPENT of your sin and give your entire heart back to Jesus!

Before we even think about getting into the details of this book, *God needs to shine His light in your heart!* Why do we think God is some genie whose lamp we can rub as we lay in the bed with some random man "praying" that everything will work out? Sister, you have totally separated yourself from God and you are making an idol out of that job, person or thing. Isaiah 59:2 (ESV) tells us *"It's your sins that have cut you off from God. Because of your sins, he has turned away and will not listen anymore."* Did you know that even thinking badly about yourself hinders God from freely flowing in your life? You are pretty much saying that what He created is no good and worthless, which is far from the truth!

Trust me, I get it—I know that you are not perfect. But if I can be totally honest with you, a true Christian is someone who pursues Jesus and not sin. Let me say that again, a true Christian is someone who pursues Jesus and not sin. Listen to what 1 John 2:1 says.

My dear children, I am writing this to you so that you will not sin. But if anyone does sin, we have an advocate who pleads our case before the Father. He is Jesus Christ, the one who is truly righteous. He himself is the sacrifice that atones for our sins—and not only our sins but the sins of all the world. And we can be sure that we know him if we obey his commandments. If someone claims, "I know God," but doesn't obey God's commandments, that person is a liar and is not living in the truth. But those who obey God's word truly show how completely they love him. That is how we know we are living in him. Those who say they live in God should live their lives as Jesus did."

So, if we really say that we love Jesus, then it will not end with the couple of words that we uttered when we were four. It will be a daily-waking-up and living for Jesus attitude. A daily death to ourselves, our emotions, our feelings, our thoughts, what that crazy auntie said, whoever else said and submitting our hearts to Jesus! It is no longer about you! It is no longer about what you thought you were going to do when you "grew up." It is no longer becoming the "doctor" your family is trying to force you to be when you know good and well God has called you in another direction!

"If you want to be my disciple, you must hate everyone else by comparison--your father and mother, wife and children, brothers and sisters--yes, even your own life. Otherwise, you cannot be my disciple." (Luke 14:26)

You see, the scripture says "by comparison." So, if your pastor is telling you to do something or your mama is telling you to be something, but God is tugging on your heart to do something else, we have to make sure our wise counsel is in line what the Lord is telling us to do.

I recall when we first moved from Atlanta, Georgia, to Jackson, Mississippi, about three months after we got married. Everyone thought we were crazy! The Lord told us to leave the church we were attending and it was hard! Our "wise" counsel told us we were going to be broke, living at home with our parents and divorced within a year. Well, almost five years into our marriage we founded the worldwide Pinky Promise organization that encourages women to honor God with their life and body. We also founded The Gathering Oasis, a growing church in Midtown, Atlanta, GA; gave birth to a beautiful son named Logan, we have a wonderful family and a great marriage. Do we get tested? Of course we do! Is it hard to be married to my husband sometimes? Umm, yes. My husband has a very strong "command man-leader" type of personality, so I get to balance him out! But the point of the story is this, if we listened to our supposed "wise" counsel we would not be where we are today.

We were not at peace with what they were telling us. We felt like they were trying to control us and keep us in a box. God was calling us out of the box and into the world to preach the gospel of Jesus. If I can be totally honest, this is my issue with "mentors." Some people run to their mentor or "wise" counsel more than they run to God. Over time and if you are not careful, the mentor could hinder your walk because he or she replaces God in their mentees life. So, if you have an issue, you run to your mentor. If you are not sure what to do, you run to your mentor. What happened to running to the feet of Jesus? What happened to spending hours in His presence, fasting and praying until He answers you? Hear me out, if you have a healthy, godly relationship with your mentor, I am not knocking it, but just make sure you are putting nothing and no one before Jesus.

Personally, I never had a mentor. My mentor has always been the Holy Spirit and He is the BEST one out there and a wonderful teacher. Also, of course my husband has been a wonderful leader. If we are so dependent on a human, we will be led by their plans and not the plans of the Lord.

So, if you are not willing to "die" to yourself and die to what everybody else says about you, you may not be ready to be a true disciple of Christ. I always say that if you want to be free from people, then plan on getting tested with people. They will talk crazy about you, treat you badly and start rumors. And, if you can get to the point where you are clinging to God and forgiving them for talking badly about you, then you are in the beginning stages of being free from people.

Remember, God cannot take you into your purpose if you are so worried and concerned about what everybody else thinks of you! People's opinions and feelings are constantly subject to change! It seems like the bigger our ministry grows; the more people come out of the woodwork and say extremely hateful things to us. They find reasons to not like us and complain about "this" or "that." Do I care? Absolutely not. It's not that I'm not humble enough to receive correction, it is just that I have a team of about five or six people that are around me and are constantly correcting me, including my husband, and we are one flesh. These people have been in my life for years and they truly know me. They know my heart. They have known me from when I was without Christ and now they see me walking with Him. I have wise counsel checking me. So, why would I listen to a hater online who wishes they had a ministry, who maybe struggling with insecurity to such a degree they create fake profiles to bash our name? Now, did this used to bother me? Yes it did! But, what if I crumbled every time a person said something bad about me? What about you? Are you experiencing some backlash from people? Use the bricks thrown at you to build a beautiful house with a foundation of Christ.

About eight years ago (2005), before I grew up and matured in Christ. I viewed people hating me as an opportunity to work out my love muscle and forgive others. I learned that everybody is not for me. I learned people will search for a weakness in me and try to expose it to make themselves feel better. Honestly, it breaks my heart. My heartbeat is that all women would come together and operate as the body of Christ, loving, encouraging and building each other up! **No one benefits when the body of Christ is so divided, with everybody hating each other!** So, I ask you this question, where do you fall in the scheme of things? Do you search to find flaws in others so you can expose them or are you on the other side—forgiving, growing and really desiring true intimacy with God? It is time for us to seriously sit before God and tell Him we are jealous, bitter and mad; that we are depressed, frustrated and impatient. Do you realize that God can work with the truth? He can work with someone who is willing to cast their cares onto Him because He cares about them!

I recall serving in about five ministries at church and being really active. I had cut off my random boyfriend and I was really focusing on living for Jesus. Then, one of the leaders in the church started a really nasty rumor about me. I was shocked because I had barely spoken to this man and then he was telling all of the other men who were serving as well! The gossip became so bad the senior pastor found out and invited me to sit down in a meeting with him. I get to the meeting and I did not know what was going on! When the pastor told me, I laughed because I was so confused! "Wait, huh? What do you mean? Is this a joke?" These guys are supposed to be my "brothers" in Christ and they are bashing my name! I had to learn the first step in being free from people-bondage is to forgive them. You have to forgive them sis. Forgive whoever has hurt you, from the parent who was not there, to the boyfriend who broke your heart, to your husband who lied to you, to your friend that hurt you.

I am reminded of Matthew 6:15 which says, "But if you refuse to forgive others, your Father will not forgive your sins."

I don't know about you, but that scares me! I fear God and I need to make sure we are on the same page at all times! I know I am not perfect, but I also know when I am walking in the flesh versus walking in the Spirit. I want to make sure that I am intentional about walking in the Spirit. So, I have learned to practice forgiving people who bash my name. So now, that forgiveness muscle has gotten really strong and what used to bother and hurt me does not bother and hurt me anymore. You may feel like you are not at that place yet— be patient. *If you continually choose life and choose forgiveness, it will come.* Sometimes, you just have to set your heart on the truth that God is greater than this world and its attacks. Tell God, by faith, you will forgive whomever for whatever and believe that your feelings will catch up later.

As you continue to read, my prayer is you search your heart and let God rip out anything that is not like Him. My prayer is that you allow for Him to wreck what you thought you knew about half-way living for Jesus and really give Him your entire heart. My prayer is you represent Jesus Christ in your words, thoughts, actions, mindset, heart and life. My prayer is you stop bullying people and start loving them. My prayer is you do not quit on God because He has such a beautiful plan for you. My prayer is you hang in there through the tests because they are only making you better.

CHAPTER 2

The Crown

Why did I call this book Dusty Crowns? Proverbs 12:4 says that "A worthy wife is a crown for her husband, but a disgraceful woman is like cancer to his bones." Even if you are single, I am reminded how God is married to us through Jesus Christ when Jesus reconciled us back to Him, and the Maker is now our husband (Isaiah 54:5). So, whether you are single or married, this book applies to you. Wherever you go and whatever you do you are representing Jesus and/or your earthly husband. Consider what your crown is saying about your life? I do not know about you, but I want to make sure when people encounter me, they see Jesus. For example, if you were at a gala and you saw a man wearing a beautiful gold crown with beautiful precious jewels and diamonds on his head, you would automatically think: "I wonder who he is?" As he walked around, he was very calm and collected. When he spoke, wisdom came out of his heart. Then, if you saw a woman walk into the gala with a mini skirt, fish net stockings, dyed blue and pink hair while wearing a see-through bra, you may quickly come to the conclusion that she's "rebellious, loud, and distracting." As she stood up, everyone watched in horror as she walked to the microphone and she chomped her gum and cussed out the entire crowd.

Which one are you? When you walk in the room—is there something so classy about your demeanor or is there something loud and rebellious about you? **Either way, your presence is making a statement when you walk into the room.** So, how do you dress? Do you like to wear clothes that reveal all of your goodies because if "you got it, you should flaunt it," right? No. We must rise above the pressures from society that says, "Less is more." Some of us are praying for a godly man, but your attire continues to attract little Johnny from around the corner whose only desire is to sleep with you. *We must remember that whatever you show, a man will think you will share with him.*

I recall for years, I wore super short, shorts and tops that were very low cut. I wore those clothes because I did not feel good about myself. I found value and worth in the attention I received from guys. I craved attention from men because I went so many years feeling *rejected and empty.* You may have heard my story in my first book, *Pink Lips and Empty Hearts*, but I was given up for adoption right from the hospital. My birth mom was only eighteen years old and was attending a boarding school when she gave birth to me. I was born in 1982 and back then, her catholic background and culture was not accustomed to raising children as a single parent. So, I went into a foster home for a few months. Then two families were interested in adopting me. The foster home gave the biracial family a "first look" at me because I am Polish, German, English and African American. They felt I would be a better fit with their family because I looked more like the members of the family. Nonetheless, they passed on me because the foster agency said I might have cerebral palsy because I was extremely stiff and I cried a lot.

The agency called my now parents and they were so excited! My mom screamed, "I will take her! I don't care what is wrong, she has been mine all along." It is seriously typical of my mother, she is a pretty unconditional, loving, warm person. I always compare her to Mother Theresa! Nonetheless, in order to feel good about myself, I wore clothes that showed off my body and I did not think twice about throwing on a pair of "booty shorts" or a little tank top with no bra. I never considered that I was actually causing men to stumble around me because of my choice in clothes. I was so insecure, so broken, so searching to be beautiful. This continued until I started to get serious about my walk with the Lord. As I gave my heart to Jesus, little by little He would convict me about my clothes.

You see, my clothes only reflected with was really going on in my heart. **I was broken inside**. I needed attention to feel good about myself. Each morning, I would wake up and ask the Lord what should I wear for the day and over time, I started to get rid of clothes that showed more than I was willing to share. During this period in my life I met my husband and, at this point, I thought I was pretty classy. I had another thing coming! At the time, I lived in New York and I flew into Atlanta to visit him. I had a long maxi dress with a spaghetti strap V-neck top portion. I was not showing cleavage because I really do not have any being a B-cup and I thought it was totally classy! AND it was a maxi dress so it was long! So, while we were out shopping with his family, Cornelius asked me to put a jean jacket on over my dress or put a tank top on under it. *"Huh?! That TOTALLY ruins my outfit! Why would I put a tank top on? I'm not even showing much"* as I started to argue and rebel in my heart. Cornelius said to me that it causes him to stumble because the V-neck was such a deep cut that it left little to the imagination. He said, "I do not want my woman walking around wearing clothes like that. She represents me when we step out together."

Then, the light clicked on— ah, I get it!

Even though we were only courting, we were headed towards marriage and when people saw us together, either we were setting a good example or a bad. So, for me, I did not want to cause him or any other men or other women to stumble?

You might be asking yourself, "How can I cause another woman to stumble?" I could wear something and she may be looking to me as the example. She may be thinking, "Because Heather wore it, it is ok to wear."

Or, if you have younger women around you—they may look up to you in every single way. If you are wearing next to nothing and you are posting those photos on Instagram, guess what? She is going to post the same photos on there as well. People are watching you, whether you believe it or not and you ARE influencing them. You are an example to someone, somewhere.

Now, this is not some law that I am putting in place to tell you to dress classy. All I am asking is this: "What is the Lord saying about what you are wearing?" **You are His crown.** You represent Him. You can actually ruin your witness when you think, act and dress a certain way. The last thing I want to do is to push someone away from Jesus just solely because of my choice of clothes.

Proverbs 12:4 tells us "An excellent wife is the crown of her husband, but she who brings shame is like rottenness to his bones."

How can you bring shame to your husband? Your spiritual husband, (God) or your earthly husband? The bible tells that God is married to us (Isaiah 54:4). Not in the earthly sense, but in the fact that He sent His only son, Jesus Christ, to the earth to die for our sins. He did this to fulfill His covenant, reminding us He is absolutely married to us and committed to us in every way.

Back then, covenants could only be broken by death. Because Jesus lives forever, we continually have a covenant with Him through the blood shed on the cross, and that convent can never be broken. The same is true for our earthly husband. When you get married, it is supposed to be committed and permanent, only to be broken by death.

So, what does your crown look like? Is it tarnished, mangled or damaged? Are you dressing to match your crown? I know you have a beautiful heart, but it is hard to see your heart when your clothes are so distracting to others. Or, is your heart not so right and you picked up this book because someone gave it to you and you just felt led to read it? Either way, it is time to get real about this walk with the Lord. It is time to quit playing games. It is time to really give your entire heart and life to Jesus.

One day, you will hear footprints coming down the hall on your last day on this earth. Those footprints will either be accompanied by singing and worship from the angels ushering you into heaven or screaming, torment with demons ushering you into hell. We cannot afford to keep playing around with our faith in Jesus Christ. We cannot afford to wear the crown of satan and quote scripture like he does. You say you love Jesus, but you continue to chase after satan's sons; wear clothes producing lust; talk and act like the world; listen to the world's music and think like this world! No wonder you do not desire God! You are filled with carnal passions.

The invisible crown you wear on your head is powerful because it shows your headship. It shows who you really belong to. Well, who is it? Ask yourself the question right now. If you were to die right now and leave this earth, would you go to heaven or would you go to hell? If you think you would go to hell, put this book down and repent of your sins. You do not know if you will be alive in the next five minutes. The Lord Jesus is calling you back to Him and it is bigger than what you wear and how you think. But, how you think and what you wear is birthed from your heart. You have to understand that the rotten fruit on your tree is produced because of a rotten root. It is time to get our foundation right.

I remember when I first got saved and gave my heart to Jesus. I was sitting in a church service and I cried the entire service. I felt pressure, like I was being reminded of my past and how terrible I was as a person. I felt rejected, condemned, judged and broken. As I cried my eyes out during the service, I turned to my best friend, Delan, and I told her how I felt. I said, "God is reminding me of my past and how much He hates me." She quickly corrected me, "No, Heather! That's not God who is condemning you, that's satan." She continued to encourage me about how God convicts me and brings me to Him, but satan makes me feel guilty and worthless.

So, I walked down the aisle that day at that church conference and I poured my heart out to God at the altar. I became married to Him and this HUGE burden was lifted. I felt safe. I was not perfect and I knew there was going to have to be a lot of "working out my salvation" (*Philippians 2:12 (KJV), "Wherefore, my beloved, as ye have always obeyed, not as in my presence only, but now much more in my absence, work out your own salvation with fear and trembling.")* because I had so much stuff in my past, but I was committed to Jesus and the journey. I was sick and tired of trying to figure out my life and I was continuing to hit rock bottom. I wanted more for myself and more for life.

I encourage you today, do not wait for a sermon to walk down the aisle to give your heart to Jesus or to decide to live for Him for real. Drop to your knees right now and pour your heart out to Jesus. *Get back to the heart of worship and dance with Jesus again.* Stop entertaining and dancing with this world. God has a plan for your life. He has a plan. I am telling you He has a plan for you and some of you are running. You are afraid God is going to force you to do something you do not want to do or give up some loser boyfriend you should not be with anyway. Some of you have such a jacked up past you think our Savior is not big enough to free you from it. Some of you are married, but you treat your husband so badly that even you are surprised he is still with you.

It is time to get back to the *heart of worship.* If you are attending a church that gives no conviction and you find yourself entertaining sin, maybe it is time to find another church. If you are bored with reading the bible, it is most likely because you are busy reading Facebook™ or busy watching the news. You see, you desire whatever you give your attention to on a regular basis. So, look over your life. What needs to change? Make a list and check it twice. Tell God you will trust Him, this journey and His timing.

CHAPTER 3

God's Timing

God's timing is one of the hardest areas to truly trust God in because you are constantly bombarded by the world. What the world tries to convince you of its timing. It starts when you are a child. You cannot "wait" to grow up and be "big" and live by your own rules as an early teen. Then, at the age of fifteen, there is this impatience, "When do I get my drivers permit/license game." Then, when you are about sixteen or seventeen years old, you cannot WAIT to move out of the house and go off to college. You sit in school, irritated at your teachers, the school complaining about the journey. Then, you finally get to college, move out and you realize the grass is not quite as green as you thought it would be on the other side. Now, you have adult bills and you have to pay for your lifestyle. While in college, you cannot wait to finish, move away and get into the "real world." You are trying to get a boyfriend because you feel like everybody else is in a relationship and you want to be in one. You graduate and you get into the real world and, if you are single, your mind and your family is reminding you to "hurry up and get married because your clock is ticking," which is a lie because you are only twenty-one. Then, you finally get married and you are trying to get pregnant for three and four years and, for some reason, you cannot conceive. So, then there is a waiting game for child. When you finally have a child and they are newborns you cannot wait for them to walk. Then, become independent.

Do you see the vicious cycle? We are so discontent with our portion that we are constantly looking to the next season in our life to feel fulfilled.

Sometimes, we feel like if we were married, or if we worked here or there, or if we had kids, or if we had more money, then we would be happier. We automatically think we would be happier somewhere else doing something else, but the reality is this: **those seasons carry their tests and trials as well.** And each season will prepare you for the next season of your life. So, get your mind off of where you wish you should be and put your eyes on Jesus.

Some of us get impatient with God and we run out ahead of Him and we get a boyfriend out of season and then it does not work out. Then, your heart is broken and you should have said goodbye at hello. If I can be totally honest, I once got into a relationship with someone and I knew I was not ready. I had just broken up with an ex and I jumped into this relationship literally a day later. But, he was cute, it was exciting and I hated to be single, so I started to date him. I had no peace about him, but in my prayer time (yes, my prayer time) I told the Lord I would do everything I knew to make things right and live according to His word. Did that happen? No. After about six months we ended up disobeying God in every way and our flesh led our relationship. I repented, but still tried to make it work and I began to put this guy over God. Then, the guy began to treat me like I was not good enough for him and told me I needed to go back to school or do something else to increase my value. Crazy, right? So now, my heart is broken, I have a new soul tie and I am mad at God that yet another relationship did not work out. Instead of really being focused on what God wants me to do, I am dealing with heartbreak. I am distracted and bitter. It was not my season for that relationship or even that person. He was a great guy, he just was not my future husband. So, just because he looks good on paper, does not mean he is the right guy. You have to be led by the Lord and not your lonely, my "clock-is-ticking" emotions.

If you are single, you may be struggling with trusting God's timing and remember this: satan is *after your mindset* and *he is after your womb*. He wants you to think that you will be like sister so and so and be single your whole life. He wants you to think that you will never get married. He wants you to think that you will be too old to have kids. He wants you to believe his stupid lies. If you believe his lies, you will be way too wrapped up and distracted from what God called you to do. You will serve in church, but deep down your heart will hurt and you will grow frustrated.

As you serve in church, little unsaved Johnny from around the corner will be pushing up on you. And since you do not get attention from those Christian men, you may give into little Johnny's advances. But, little Johnny has AIDS. He just does not look like it—because he is so fine to you. Or, little Johnny has an STD that will eat away at your womb. Then, when you do leave that loser and get married, you have to deal with a lingering STD you did not realize you had. You see, if satan can mess up your womb, you will not "be fruitful and multiply", producing children after the likeness of Jesus. You will not raise them up to know who Jesus is if satan can get rid of your womb. We all know God is a Healer and He can heal any problem or issue, but what if there is no healing? What if you have to live with it forever all due to thirty seconds with little Johnny? If you knew the destination of your sin, I can assure you, you would never do it. You would not even look for a minute at little Johnny!

And, if people are mocking you for "taking this whole Jesus thing a little far" and really working on being a proper crown for Jesus, some guys may not want to date you. When you decide to stand for what is right, some of those guys will say that you are "taking this Jesus thing really deep, you cover too much and you are ready to get married," as if doing this were a bad thing. They can pick that up. GOOD!

Do not apologize for wanting to be a wife and not a girlfriend. You encourage a man to think about his motives and his vision. If you have a "girlfriend" mindset you will do just about anything without a ring. You will play house, wear whatever and will not challenge him to measure up and step up to the plate. So, do not get mad if the guy runs off to dusty, trashy crowns who have low or no standards. *Hold onto your standards because your future husband will be looking for a godly wife.*

Same goes if you are married. It is never worth it to begin an emotional or physical tie from someone that is not your spouse. I heard of this story in Georgia as I wrote this chapter and it broke my heart. A wife and a mother of two little boys shot herself in the head and killed herself while her husband was in another room and her children were playing outside. She killed herself because she committed adultery against her husband and she could no longer live with herself. So, because of her initial selfish act, she left her husband broken, widowed and a single parent to two small children. It is an absolutely heartbreaking situation. My question to you is: If you knew the ultimate destination of stepping out on your husband, would you do it? If an ex or a co-worker is pushing up on you and you are married, you have to remember that if you were supposed to be with them, you would be married to them and not your spouse. If you are even thinking about stepping out on your spouse, it is NOT worth it. Fight back. Deactivate Facebook, quit your job, or move to another department. Do whatever it takes to protect your marriage because the thing is this: you like the adventure, you like the unknown and you like the attention that he gives you. Do not be deceived, God is not giving you that attention; satan himself is giving it to you. And he is using your co-worker or your ex-boyfriend from Facebook to plant seeds in your heart so he can ruin your marriage, your life, even an entire generation of your seed and so much more. **It is never, ever, ever worth it**. Honestly, marriage can be downright hard sometimes and the last thing you need is an unnecessary person in the mix of things. He may be fun now, but once he starts catching feelings and gets crazy while trying to force you to leave your husband, you will soon realize it was never worth it.

In the early stages of our marriage, there were even times where I thought, "Gosh, life was so much easier when I was single and it was just me." But then, I quickly rebuke myself, put on my big girl pants and submit to my husband as He submits to Jesus.

Maybe, relationships are not your issue, but truly trusting God concerning your purpose and WHEN to step out on God's timing. Some of you are stepping out even into ministry and you are finding yourself worn out and tired. You are not even graced for that season yet but you are trying to rush something and you are coming up exhausted and tired.

For example, God told me my purpose in 2003 after we had a date night together. He told me that I would travel all over this world, preach the gospel of Jesus and that millions of people will come into the knowledge of WHO He is through me and my husband's ministry. So, after He told me, what if I stepped out to start a ministry at that moment? That ministry would not have gotten very far. I was so immature in my walk with the Lord and I did not have the character to step out and help anyone! I needed to be faithful in the small things, or the people who were around me during that season would not have received what I was giving. I was far from ready in stepping out to start anything. I needed to step into my bible and that is about it. I was not ready for a ministry! I was impatient, hurt, bitter, unforgiving, tired, worried and confused about God's timing. I did not need any human confusing my life any more than it already was. I needed daily encounters with Jesus Christ. I needed His leading. I needed His direction in the small stuff before I even thought about stepping into ministry! There is a time under the sun for the seasons in your life. Some of you are not ready for a husband, kids, a certain job, a certain direction, a certain ministry. It is just not time yet. If you were to get it now, you would most likely ruin your relationships. You would pour your confused mindset into a ministry and confuse other people. Sometimes, you need a wealth of experience before God opens those doors. I did not see any part of what God told me from 2003-2011.

In 2011, I endured a series of tests, including losing my step-dad to a sudden death (my dad passed in 2000 from a heart attack), my nephew committing suicide, having a miscarriage and my friend died of a brain aneurysm. All of this happened in a month's time. This nearly broke me. In addition to that, my car was taken and given back to the bank. I was paying the note every month and I was getting pretty close to paying it off, but the dealer I purchased the car from in New Jersey sold me a car with a dirty title. The car was repossessed by the previous owner's employee and the employee called it in as stolen, completely unaware that it was taken back by his boss. Nonetheless, the old owner never called to update the title and they somehow sold the car to me a year later. Crazy, right? Well, we prayed earlier that year that the Lord would strip us from anything He did not want us to have at the time. Well, I literally was being ripped from any type of comfort I had. I felt like I was in such a dry, broken season in my life.

So, God placed it on my heart to start blogging. He encouraged me to start sharing what He was birthing in me and taking out of me. Somehow, out of nowhere, I looked up and I had over one million views on my blog within a few months. I was so confused! How did these people find me? I was surprised that people even cared to hear what God placed on my heart. To this day I am completely shocked that people even show up at our speaking engagements. I absolutely know that it is God who is increasing our ministries numbers and nothing else. I am so humbled because I remember those years where it was just me and Jesus. Then Jesus, me and my hubby. Now, it is Jesus and my little family. After another 6-8 months blogging, I started Pinky Promise, The organization that encourages women to honor God with their life and body. I started it from a bracelet. I made one of those "WWDJ" style bracelets, instead mine said PINKY PROMISE, and they sold like crazy online! I was not planning on starting a ministry from a bracelet. I simply made a bracelet and put it online to encourage people to live for Jesus. I never sought to put my name out there. I just wanted to live for Jesus and please Him. Even now, with the speaking engagements, books and all the open doors, I look at Jesus and I am like, "you sure? I'm really just a messed up woman from Brooklyn, Michigan. I am thankful for everything You do but sometimes I do not even feel adequate in doing all of these things." Then, Jesus whispers to my heart, **"You are right, Heather. In your own power, ability and way, you are absolutely never ready. But, in my power, my ability and my way—I give you the strength and direction."** You see, I needed to learn this over those 9 years where I did not see any ministry fruit on my tree. I had to trust God's timing, even when I was working a "9 to 5" and developing in not stealing the paper from my old company, or using the ink to print out my bible studies or lying to my boss.

There was a TIME when I needed to work and there is a time when I needed to be developed. I am reminded of one of my favorite scriptures in Ecclesiastes 3:1 the writer tells us:

"There is a time for everything, and a season for every activity under the heavens: a time to be born and a time to die, a time to plant and a time to uproot, a time to kill and a time to heal, a time to tear down and a time to build, a time to weep and a time to laugh, a time to mourn and a time to dance, a time to scatter stones and a time to gather them, a time to embrace and a time to refrain from embracing, a time to search and a time to give up, a time to keep and a time to throw away, a time to tear and a time to mend, a time to be silent and a time to speak, a time to love and a time to hate, a time for war and a time for peace."

Do you understand that your life is laid out with purpose? There is no way I was going to see any fruit on my ministry tree. I simply was not ready. I also walked by my now husband for three years as we went to the same church. We did not need to connect three years prior to that because the Lord was working out some things in my heart. This does not mean you will all of a sudden "arrive" or be perfect when you get married; get that dream job; or even walk into your purpose. You will always have things to work on!

But, what about my past?

CHAPTER 4

Your Past

"This means that anyone who belongs to Christ has become a new person. The old life is gone; a new life has begun!" (2 Corinthians 5:17)

Let's clear up this area quickly. You may be feeling guilty about your past because you were not perfect, or maybe you are not a "virgin" or whatever else may have happened. Did you know Jesus died for those who have a past? He is not surprised by the decisions you made so, from sister to sister, you have got to let go of whatever from your past is holding you in bondage. Each year, it seems like you just push your hurts and troubles under a rug. Hurt after hurt after hurt. You plaster a smile on your face that says everything is "ok" but deep down, it is so far from it. You feel empty on the inside. The problem with pretending is it leaves you empty inside. We push our hurts and pains under this huge rug and then over time, the sin from our past begins to seep into our jobs, relationships and heart today. We try to hide it. We try to fix it with our own ability. We try to do all of these things, but we continually come up empty because of sin.

When we sin, we separate ourselves from God. Then, because we think that God is mad at us for our sin, we stop going to church, we stop reading the bible and we stop pursuing a relationship with Him. You feel like, *"what is the point when I keep messing up?"* The point is this: *You cannot earn your relationship with God.* Your "feel good" or "not-so-feel good" emotions **have nothing to do with God loving you or not.** When my son Logan manages to break open the remote and put a battery in his mouth, I run and snatch the battery away from him. (Since then, we hide the remotes in an area in which he cannot reach.) Do I hate him? No. Am I mad at him? No! Do I still love him? Of course! He was just making a poor decision and I had to discipline him by saying, "No!"

Some of you are making poor decisions and God closes your doors, shuts it down and "pulls the battery away from you." And although Logan cries because he doesn't understand, like a good parent, I do what is best for him.

Hebrews 12:6 says: "For the LORD disciplines those he loves, and he punishes each one he accepts as his child."

God is trying to show you the way you are supposed to go in this life so do not get mad when he disciplines your sin! He is screaming into your heart and conscience, saying that you are GOING THE WRONG WAY!! Turn AROUND! Come back to my HEART. I want ALL OF YOU!

So, what do you do when satan reminds you of your past? Do you agree and allow it to overwhelm you or do you talk back to the struggles? When satan and his little demons try to mess with me, I remind him of his past and his future. I tell him that he is just mad because I am made in the image of Jesus and because I belong to HIM and satan is mad because he cannot wipe me out. I ask him how it "feels" to have to get permission from God to attack Christians. I ask him how it "feels" to get kicked out of heaven. I remind him that he is going to burn in hell forever! See, you cannot skip around fearing your past, those crazy thoughts or whatever else! Satan is real. Hell is real. The enemy is real! Put on that armor and fight back!

If you had a small peek into the plans God has for you, you would delete that random (a random is a man you know you will never marry, but you date them because you are bored or lonely) and you would be so focused on what God wants you to do because you know that due season always comes. You will not pop off at the mouth to your husband because you recognize your husband is a helper to God and you are your husband's helper. So when you cut up in the house, it affects your very purpose. You also will not chase down those "one way street" friendships. You see, those people who left you or those people you are begging to stay fit your dysfunction. They fit your pain. They fit your hurt. They fit where you see yourself now. **But they are not going where you are going**. So, if you do not cut them off, God will help you. He is much more concerned about the plans He has for you than you having a pair of particular thighs in your bed or a girl's night on Friday. Do you not want the thighs and friends that God has for you?! I know that I did. *I did not have time to have a pair of dusty thighs that should not be in my bed.* See, I had been there, done that, and literally wrote the book about it. I wanted who GOD had for me and I refused to settle. This meant that if I needed to be single for the rest of my life, I was going to do just that. Then, I looked up after a season of singleness and I met my husband. I did not even want a boyfriend at the time. I was sick and tired of playing games. But, I learned this, God is not working according to our timing—**He is on His own timing**. And when He brings two people together, He is bringing them together with purpose. He is bringing them together to bring Him glory. So, it was bigger than me having a pair of legs in my bed and comfort at night. It was bigger than sex.

God had ministry in mind when He brought me together with my husband.

You may be thinking, why would God use my spouse or why would God use me? I have such a terrible past and I am afraid of what others will think of me. **Honey, you better dust off that crown and lift your head up.** People are going to talk about you whether you are doing something good or something bad. Either way, make sure you are living for Jesus and seek to please Him, not a bunch of humans.

I remember when I first started talking about God on social media. I remember someone said to me, "How are you saved? I remember when you used to be like this and that. Don't forget where you came from." Translation: *your life convicts me of my own sin and I do not like the idea of you growing, so I am going to bash you to make you come down to my level.* Before God even showed me that revelation, I thought to myself: "I MAY have been like that, BUT, I am not like that anymore. Why are you still the same?" But, I did not think that was the most encouraging, godly thing to think or say.

Nonetheless, I remembered what Jesus did for me on the cross. What He did was so intimate between you and Him that no hurt, broken person can come in between the bond you have. He saved you. *He saved you. He saved you.* Some human's mere words cannot destroy the faith you have in the cross. So, in so many words, **people will hate on you**. They will not understand you. They will not get this newfound walk with the Lord. They will not understand why you want to put clothes on and actually dress classy. They will not understand why you want to wait to kiss until you get married. They will try to convince you to date randoms and say, "how will you know what you want unless you go out with a bunch of men?" Last time I checked, *I did not need my heart broken to know how it feels.* I do not need to be cheated on, lied to, and broken, in order to see what I want in a spouse.

If you want to get free from your past and free from the bondage of people, get prepared to go on a journey. This journey may not be especially pretty either because in order to be free from people, you have to be free from the things *they say about you.* So, guess what? Get prepared to hear gossip about you and to run into tests and trials. Remember this: 1 Peter 1:7 *"These trials are only to test your faith, to show that it is strong and pure. It is being tested as fire tests and purifies gold -- and your faith is far more precious to God than mere gold. So if your faith remains strong after being tried by fiery trials, it will bring you much praise and glory and honor on the day when Jesus Christ is revealed to the whole world."*

Is our crown brilliant and humbled by God? Completely ready for His leading and guiding? Or are we still holding onto our past and allowing it to define us?

CHAPTER 5

What kind of Diamonds are on Your Crown?

Cubic Zirconia vs. Authentic Diamond

According to the Diamond Source of Virginia, there are three different types of diamonds produced.

1. **Expensive Diamonds:** Diamonds are typically formed deep beneath the earth's surface. They are made up of pure carbon, which has been placed under immense pressure for millions of years. The intense heat produced due to this pressure hardens the carbon. Natural diamonds are rare to find and are very expensive.

2. **Synthetic Diamonds:** These diamonds are produced synthetically in high pressure, high temperature processes which

stimulates the condition of the earth's mantle, but are man-made.

3. **Cubic Zirconia:** This alternative technique is chemical vapor deposition, several non-diamond materials, which include cubic zirconia, are diamond stimulates, resembling diamonds in appearance and many properties.

How can you tell what is a fake diamond and what is a real diamond? Special gemological techniques have been developed to distinguish natural versus synthetic diamonds.

Now, what does this have to do with you? It has to do with the diamonds that are on your crown. So, which diamonds are you carrying on your crown?

Are you a cubic zirconia? You resemble a Christian in appearance and many properties, but when the gemologist (Holy Spirit) checks you out, He shows you that you only appear to be a diamond or you are pretending to be a diamond. You see, it is not just enough to say you are a Christian. There must be some fruit on your tree.

I have this costume jewelry, cubic zirconia bracelet and I will most likely lose it within the next year. Not on purpose, but just because it only cost me a few dollars. I do not place as much value on the costume jewelry and if it were to be appraised, I would most likely get about one dollar for it. You see, cubic zirconia has not been through anything and it runs from the heat from the earth's mantle. When tests and trials come its way they refuse to suffer for Jesus. They show up at church every now and then but it is all a show. Or, are there synthetic diamonds on your crown? Synthetic diamonds are made artificially. It is a step up from the cubic zirconia. You have given your life to Jesus, but you still hold onto some men, things and people. You are the lukewarm in between diamond, and you are neither hot nor cold. You cannot be totally radical about Jesus because of what others will say.

> *"But since you are like lukewarm water, neither hot nor cold, I will spit you out of my mouth!"* *(Revelations 3:16)*

When you hear a word, you are excited about it and then the devil snatches the word from you the second you get tested. You may fight back here and there, but because you are a synthetic diamond, you always give in to satan and you go back to what makes you comfortable. These types of diamonds are man-made. They care about what others think of them and are in people bondage. Or lastly, are you an expensive diamond? These diamonds are made deep in the earth and a volcano is necessary to bring it close to the surface. Can I be honest with you? *This diamond has been through hell on earth and still is determined to live for Jesus.* When things come your way you overcome the temptation and you sit and trust God. You tell God you are not going anywhere and you really live it out. These diamonds suffer and nobody can see you being developed deep in the earth's mantle. You are constantly obeying God and you pursue Him and not sin. You are privately obeying Jesus when nobody else is looking and one day, through tests and trials (volcano) you will be pushed into the top of the earth's mantle for all to see.

In order to be a diamond, there is a process that has to take place. There is a private process of being broken before the Lord and allowing Him to develop you into His image. No human, your mama, some pastor or your mentor cannot take credit for your growth because you know without a shadow of doubt it was God who saved you, healed you and made you whole. As a real diamond, nobody sees you privately obeying God. Nobody sees God cutting and wrecking you. When the pressure builds up in the earth's mantle, eruptions occur and God begins to BURN out anything that is not like Him. He begins to set you apart and you start to lose pretend friends and relationships. God begins to move you along the right path.

First Peter 3:14 says: "But even if you suffer for doing what is right, God will reward you for it."

You suffer. Your entire perspective is focused on Christ and what He wants to do in your life. The volcano has burned your ideas; visions, dreams and mindset and now you let God show you HIS ideas, visions, dreams and mindset.

So, the theme of this book is getting ready for your heavenly crown, so what kind of crown are you wearing? Is it dusty? Does your life represent the crown, jewels and diamonds on your head?

Is the fruit on your tree saying that the only crown you really want is to be a wife on this earth while totally neglecting your spiritual crown? Does the fruit on your tree say the only crown you want is to climb the corporate ladder? Does the fruit on your tree say you only want the praise of people? Matthew 16:24 says *"Then Jesus said to his disciples, "If any of you wants to be my follower, you must turn from your selfish ways, take up your cross, and follow me."*

You see, I did not truly see my life until I let go of it. Until we truly pay the real cost, we will not see our purpose and our plan. So many of us have more hope in the UPS delivering a package to us than we do the Lord. After you order your item, you wait for the tracking number, you constantly go online to see where your item is located and you get excited because you know exactly when the item will arrive to your house. Your hope is in the UPS man pulling up and knocking on the door and giving you your package. You have MORE faith in that then you do Jesus. The one who created the heavens and the earth.

So, ask yourself this question: What kind of diamond am I? If you feel like you are not real or genuine, fall onto your knees and ask God to make His word so real in your *heart that you do not want anything or anyone else.* Note that you will not ever be perfect and you will constantly be a work in progress as you pursue Jesus and instead of chasing down sin, you will chase down Jesus.

So, let go of the funky attitude. Let go of your old ways. Let go of your hurt. Let go of your pain and lay it at the feet of Jesus. *Put this book down now and go cry out to Him.* Tell Him that you are fake, that you pretend, that you hate people, that you are hurting, that you are broken!

Did you know God can work with that? He can work with a person who is intentional about living for Him. He can work with someone who repents daily of their sins. He can work with someone who really is trying to change. So, miss "know it all," let go of your control.

CHAPTER 6

Your Attitude: Miss Know it All

If I can just be real with you sister, no man wants a woman who thinks that she knows everything. If you are skipping around with this "independent" spirit you will end up being single your whole life or, in a marriage where you are running that man. Meaning, God will have a hard time getting through to your husband because he is so distracted by his wife who is trying to lead him and forcing the relationship out of proper order.

Men are natural problem solvers. They want to "fix" whatever is making you unhappy. They are wired to protect and cover you. When they hear your rants, they want to help solve the problem and be your "Spiderman" protecting you from the "bad guy." So, help me out sisters, how can he rescue you if you have *already rescued yourself?* This is a sure way to run a man away by constantly nagging him and acting like you are a walking dictionary, or let me bring it a little closer, a "walking bible." You know how you do sister;

because you have "been saved a little bit longer than him, so you think you need to teach him." You think because he spends time with God differently, then it is not "good enough." Who are we to compare how a man spends time with God? You need to be glad that he wants to spend time with God because some men refuse to do so.

I remember during the beginning of my marriage I used to compare my quiet time to my husband's quiet time. I turn on worship music; I spin around and dance for the Lord. I cry out, lay prostate and pour my guts out to Jesus. Then, I journal what is on my heart, study whatever God places on my heart and then, I just get quiet so the Lord can speak to me. After I get quiet, I pull out my bible and I study what I am going through or an area God places on my heart. My husband's quiet time is totally different! He sits down at his table, with his bible, notes, concordance, computer and tea. The lights are dim and it is totally quiet. There is no worship music. No spinning around. Nothing! I used to think, "What is wrong with you? **How BORING is your quiet time??** How are you even getting anything from the Lord?" I was wrong, right? Totally wrong. My husband has a very Type A- Command-Man personality and that is how he relates to God. My quiet time does not make me any better a person. I need to mind my own business and trust that God will pull on my husband's heart to spend time with Him.

If you do not tackle this "independent" attitude while you are a single woman, it is only going to get worse when you get married. You will get married, continue to run your man, then he will either rebel, hand his headship to you and be totally out of order or go into secret sins. You will wreck his confidence as a man and make him feel like he is worth nothing. Sister, only a fool tears down her own body and when you get married, you become one flesh or one unit. So, how dare you tear down that man and talk down to him? You ought to be ashamed of yourself! I am not trying to beat you down as a woman. I am trying to love you back to the Father! **You are planting some nasty seeds in your marriage and your husband has gone so deep into the cave in his heart and he is not coming out until you can respect him.**

Women always fuss at me about this when I say it, but I am still going to say it: You can easily push your man away mentally or physically. Imagine this; you bash him with your words and your nasty attitudes; you talk down to him; you refuse to let him lead; you do not submit to him; you treat your pastor better than you treat your man and you *constantly* compare him to others. Then, he goes to work and he is a manager over his department. The new coordinator recognizes his hard work and often compliments him on the hard work. She is always happy, always smiling, has a pretty face, banging body, does not know Christ, but she is always serving your husband at work. And, she is crushing on your man. **Now, just think about that for a second sister, do you not think your husband will compare her joy to your nagging?** I am not saying it is right. I am not saying it is biblical. What I am saying is you have opened a door for satan to tap dance on your marriage because of the way you treat your man. He may begin to prefer being at work than being at home. He likes how nice she is and he finally feels like the "man." And guess what? YOU opened that door into your marriage sister.

Since satan knows his time is short, knowing God will crush his head under our feet (Romans 16:20), all hell is breaking loose to make war with God's children (Revelation 12:17). If he is going down, he is going to take down as many people as possible. So he and his angels deceive the nations (Romans 20:10), incite people to sin (1 Chronicles 21:1), sow weeds into people's lives to choke the word God is trying to plant in them (Matthew 13:39). They take possession of peoples' lives. They bind people. They steal, kill and destroy. Satan's name means accuser (Zechariah 3:2). He captivates people. He plans his moves in each of our lives. (Ephesians

6:11). He is a roaring lion looking for lives to devour (1 Peter 5:8). He tests, tempts and torments people. He disguises himself as an angel of light (1 Corinthians 11:14). For a time he hinders God's work from happening (1 Thessalonians 2:18) and this is why God tells us not to "let the sun go down on your anger and do not give the Devil an opportunity" (Ephesians 4:26-27).

So, since we know all of the above, I ask you sister to do your part. Imagine this story, you love your husband. You are submitted to him, you support, encourage, and respect his leadership. You praise him publically and privately. He is not perfect but you do not focus on his issues, but his strengths, leaving his issues at the feet of Jesus. You recognize his love language and you do your best to meet his needs as the Lord helps you. You pray for him daily and you truly are working on becoming a better woman. He goes to work on Monday and meets the new coordinator that has a huge smile on her face. She is always happy, always smiling, has a pretty face, banging body and she is always serving your husband at work. She is not saved and is crushing a little bit on your man. She compliments his hard work and goes above and beyond. Your husband will recognize her hard work but he is not thinking about her because for him, his heart is back home and the doors are sealed up there.

Should a man's heart be at home even if he is getting treated badly? Of course it should be! However, one of the main reasons the divorce rate is so high is because both sides are refusing to do their part and meet the needs their spouse. So, if your husband does sense she is crushing on him, he will either fire her or move her to another department. He is not interested in losing his family and life over a silly fling or a side-chick.

I am saying your husband has a part to play because he is the leader over your home. He has a part to play in guarding his heart and casting down bad thoughts and making them obey Christ (2 Corinthians 10:5). He has a part in making sure that he is dying to his feelings and loving you. He has a part to submit his life to Jesus. **But, your husband is not reading this book. You are reading this book.** So because you are reading this book I have to encourage you to do your part sister. I have watched my entire marriage change for the better when I stopped nagging my husband and I shut up! Meaning, I stopped feeling the need to always respond and have a commentary about everything. I always had an answer for everything and I often nagged my husband and challenged his leadership. So, I learned to shut up so God could actually have a chance to speak to my husband in our peaceful home. I spoke up as the Lord led me and I learned that I did not have to *talk so much to get my point across.* Then, I watched God change my husband's heart and I could not take credit for it.

For example, my love language is touch. I would nag my husband to touch me all day long and we would get in these huge blow out arguments and he would say that "nothing is ever good enough for me." Then, I stopped nagging him and started respecting him by not constantly bringing up how I felt "unloved" in regards to touch. And, although I read all of the "mommy" books in the world, I had to learn to shut up and let my husband raise our son as well. It is not the end of the world if Cornelius uses the wrong type of body wash to bathe Logan. I had something to say about his lack of affection, the way he raised Logan and whatever else. You know how we do sisters, **we think we know everything**. Nonetheless, I grabbed a hold of God's rest. I would talk to my emotions when I saw certain situations and I started passing some tests! My husband actually said to me: "You know Heather, now that you stopped nagging me to touch you—I actually enjoy touching you more because you are not yelling at me about it." There is just something about adjusting your focus. If your focus is on this earth, you will always have something to fuss about. But, if it is focused on Jesus, you will truly be content in Him.

As I mentioned before, my love language is touch and my husband's love language is "Acts of Service." (A concept from *The 5 Love Languages* by Gary Chapman) Which means, I feel most loved when my husband is affectionate with me by holding hands, hugging and touching. My husband feels most loved when I am cleaning, washing the dishes, doing the laundry and all of that other un-fun stuff. All I want to do is curl up on a couch and cuddle with my man and he is thinking, "But there are dishes in the dishwasher, if you want to show me you love me, wash them." Yes, it is hard sometimes, but when you get married, you die to yourself, your way of thinking and your old ideas. Prayerfully, you married a man who will do the same. One-sided submission is hard but it can be done. I am reminded of 1 Peter 3: 13:

> *"Who is going to harm you if you are eager to do good? But even if you should suffer for what is right, you are blessed. "Do not fear their threats; do not be frightened." But in your hearts revere Christ as Lord. Always be prepared to give an answer to everyone who asks you to give the reason for the hope that you have. But do this with gentleness and respect, **keeping** a clear conscience, so that those who speak*

maliciously against your good behavior in Christ
may be ashamed of their slander. For it is better, if it
is God's will, to suffer for doing good than for doing
evil. (NIV)

Can I be real with you? To my single sisters, I know that marriage may look beautiful and a lot better than where you are now. You may be envious of other people who you see at church or wherever else and they seem to be really happy. Know this: If a marriage is successful, it is because the wife is dying to herself and submitting to her husband and her husband is dying to himself and submitting to Christ. There is a lot of death going on in their marriage. They die to their attitudes. They die to their old way of thinking. They die to their exes. They die to their past. They die to who they are and they take up their cross and follow Jesus Christ. So, there will be times when your current husband is not treating you as "happy" as you want to be treated. There will be times when you feel like, maybe, you are not being appreciated or honored as a wife. There will be times when you feel like your guy should communicate more with you. There will be times when you wish he was more romantic and said sweeter things to you. But the Bible says if you are suffering for doing good—or forgiving him when "you don't think" he deserves it—it is honorable to

God! The crazy thing is; we may think we are "suffering" because our man does not want to cuddle with us and there are bigger issues going on in this earth. **You have to adjust your perspective!** If you do not, then satan is going to have a field day in your life! You may pat yourself on the back and say to yourself, "well, I'm a wife and I've never cheated. Or, I have a fiancé and I've never stepped outside of our courtship." **But have your thoughts?** Did you know you could sin against God in your very thought process? Matthew 5:8 tells us: *"But I say, anyone who even looks at a woman with lust has already committed adultery with her in his heart."* So, have you sinned against your marriage in your own heart because you wished your husband was more like "your ex or some other woman's husband?" Then, you justify your thoughts because of your pity party. Is it hard to cast down those thoughts? YES! Is it hard to love the unlovable? Of course it is. I even get tempted in throwing a pity party and I attend the party in my marriage. There are times where I wish my husband would skip around and hold my hand and cuddle with me all day long. **But, will I still love him unconditionally if he does not do the things that I want him to do?** Do I truly love like Jesus commands me to love? Or, am I waiting for my man to "perform" for me to love him completely?

If we do not practice this selflessness while we are single, when we get married we will feel like our husband has to "earn our love." Not only do our husbands have to earn our love, but then we think we know more, nag him about everything and challenge every decision. If you continue down a path of challenging your man non-stop, you will find you have *wrecked* his confidence. Then, you will look up fifty years later and wonder why your marriage is exactly the same and the will of God is unfulfilled in your life. Have you seen a great president or leader standing next to a woman who was publically tearing him down? How you treat your man behind closed doors shows up publically. You may think you are putting on a show and a smile for everybody else, but we can see it in your attitude, heart towards him and his silence.

If I can be totally transparent with you, it just does not make sense to me why a woman would tear down her man. Especially if you all are married! The Bible calls you one flesh. So, let's be intentional in loving, in serving and in building up our spouses. And if you are married, look better than you did single—spiritually and physically.

CHAPTER 7

Physical Appearance

Of all the chapters I have written for this book, this chapter was difficult for me to write. It is hard for me to write because this area is so sensitive and I want to make sure I word it in a way that does not hurt you or turn you off from hearing my heart.

Alright sisters, now you know that I love you. No, really. I do love you and I have got to be honest with you about this area. I do not hear many women address this area because people do not like to step on your toes. I am not crazy about it either, but I am crazy about obeying God and He placed this area really heavy on my heart.

I know I will not always please people with what God places on my heart. However, I have to say these things because I am sick and tired of hearing men complain about these areas. These are things they may not tell you to your face, but as a sister I want to say, that sister-to-sister, we are in this together.

It is time to pull yourself together physically and work on being intentional about eating healthy, working out, combing your hair and smelling good. Why is it that we want to be attracted to our one-day spouses or we want to be attracted to our husbands, but we walk around in hair scarves and basketball shorts all day and night?

Can I be real with you? I once was not attracted to my ex. Well, there were a few guys that I was not totally attracted to, but because they looked good on "Christian paper, I settled and thought there is no way in Christ I can have a guy I am really attracted to. So, I took the scriptures and told myself I would "suffer" and *marry a guy just because he is saved and loved Jesus because I felt like my options were limited.*

Until this one day at church. I remember worshipping God and I looked up and saw a guy with his arms stretched up to heaven and brother-man was FINE! I had to take an entire moment and tell myself, "I cast down that lust!" I was so sensitive to Jesus and I only wanted to serve Him, so why am I checking out this man in church? I looked away and repented and I heard the Lord whisper into my heart: *"See Heather, there are Christian men who live for me that YOU will be attracted to. So do not feel like you have to settle. I know your desires and I have not forgotten about you."* Do you know that it FREED me to hear that? So, I broke things off with this guy I was briefly hanging out with because he totally was not my type in the world or in the kingdom. I am just saying, you understand sisters. I do not know about you, but I wanted to wake up every day and look at my husband and think, "Man, he is FINE!" Know this, it is not all about his looks. His looks are such a small piece of the picture. Because I also once dated a fine man, but he was so ugly on the inside that I could not stand to be around him. His cute smile turned dark to me.

Since you understand my perspective, I want to bring this a little bit closer to your life and be brutally honest with you: **men are visual.** Looks matter to men and you can be as beautiful as you want to be, but if you are ugly on the inside, it does not matter. Or, you can be as beautiful as it is on the inside, but you walk around with a rag on your head, in pajamas 24-7 and wearing your slippers to the store, your potential husband may walk right by you. I recall an instance when Cornelius and I were courting and we were about to go grab lunch. We had a huge birthday dinner planned that night so my hair was in pin-curls. I had a maxi dress on for lunch with my hair in pin curls and when Cornelius came to the door to greet me, I said that I was ready. He looked at me and said, "No you're not. Take those pin curls down and fix your hair." Deep down, I'm like, "WHY? There is nothing wrong with me walking out with my hair pinned!" He explained to me that when we step out together, we represent one another. He prefers a classy woman who takes care of herself physically.

Another story—now, as a wife, whenever I blow dry my hair REALLY big, I walk up to Cornelius and I flip my huge, blown out, frizzy hair back and forth and I say, "Hi! I'm Heather, would you like to go on a date with me?" And Cornelius looks at me and says no way! Of course, we are happily married, but he said if I would have gone on a first date with my hair like that, he would not have entertained the relationship any further! So, my response? "You mean to tell me you would not encourage me to get a flat iron and to work with me? We have this worldwide ministry and you would throw it all away at hello just because my hair is frizzy?" He says a simple, "yes."

Now, I know that every man is not like my husband. But, as I mentioned before, men are visual creatures. The wife is the crown of her husband and he likes a beautiful crown—inside and out. This does not mean you have to dress up in a beautiful gown everyday by no means—but what it does mean is you should wake up, get in the shower, wash those certain parts of your body that seem to produce a stronger smell, and *put on some clothes*. Although this world is temporary, people will either take you seriously or write you off because of your appearance. Of course, God can open doors that no man can close, I get it, but you have a part to play in making sure that you smell good, that you are showered and that you are dressed fit for your body type. Personally, I like to wear tops that aren't super tight and I love dresses. I know there are certain clothes that do not work for my body type because of my shape. So, find things that flow with your body type and if you cannot afford it, it is ok! Ask God to give you wisdom on how to be wise with your finances and go to Thrift Stores!

I have a friend who lives on her husband's police officer salary with her and FOUR boys! She thrift shops for their clothes and finds dresses and clothes for fifty cents! We can search for excuses to not pull ourselves together physically until we are blue in the face but with YouTube, the internet and Pinterest, we should be covered on how to do our hair, makeup and what works best with our body type.

So, sisters, stop wearing the see-through shirts that show your belly. You have to respect yourself more! What you show is what people think you will share! If you want people to take you seriously, you need to cover up your goodies.

I want you to ask yourself a question: Do I look my best? No really, do I look my best? You can think of a million and one excuses as to why you may or may not look your best and many of those reasons, I am sure are very valid. However, I want to challenge your mindset. If you were to go to a prom, you would get dressed in your absolute best. You would get your hair done, nails done, find a beautiful dress, you would shave your legs and underneath your arms and you would be intentional about looking great.

So, pounder this: *It is not that you do not know how to look your best, you simply lack the desire to look your best all the time!* Or, you may be too busy or feel like it is not a priority. And in comparison to spiritual things, it is NOT a priority. There is a balance in this thing and if you can grab ahold of it, you will even feel more confident about yourself when you are working out, smelling good and looking your best, AFTER spiritual things.

As I shared throughout this book, our hearts must be right before the Lord and we must accept Him or **we will have a face full of makeup sitting in hell.** But, since most of you understand this and you are really working on being beautiful on the inside—I want to challenge you to step your looks game up. I recall our first year of marriage. I worked from home for a software hedge accounting firm. I would wake up, pray, brush my teeth, make breakfast for me and Cornelius and I would sit down at my desk and work from about 9am-6pm, taking very few breaks. I would not shower or get dressed in the morning, I typically waited until 6 or 7pm to actually shower and get dressed into my pajamas. I would wear a hair wrap, Yoga pants and tank tops every single day. Then, one day Cornelius came home from the gym and asked me if I was going to get dressed? Huh? Why? *I do not see anyone unless I am hosting a meeting via web conference.* Why do I need to get dressed? He said, "Heather, I like to see you look nice and presentable. When I come home from meetings or the gym, I like to see you looking pretty and smelling good."

Welp, I got my tail up and got showered and dressed. Is it really worth an argument to not get dressed daily? I could have said, "Well, you married me like this—so why do I have to change?" **Well, actually—he didn't marry me like this.** When we went on dates, I got dressed in my absolute best. I made sure that my hair, makeup and clothes were on point. So, after the ring, I got a little comfortable. I mean, he will not leave me for anybody else and our marriage is permanent. Then, I got a revelation: **some woman, somewhere would LOVE to get dressed up and take her hair out of her scarf for my man.** Granted, our motivation should never be out of fear that another woman would snatch our man, but it should definitely put things into perspective. I do not want my husband to even subconsciously compare me in my PJ's all day to a woman that is intentional about looking nice. It is vital that we have flashbacks of the times when we were on our knees before the Lord, *praying for our one-day husband* and making all of these "vows" of things we would do once we get married. You know how we as women do sometimes: "Lord, when you send me my husband, I will never take him for granted. I will cook, clean up and I will not nag Him. I will be so good to your son, Lord!" Then, we get married and we gossip, yes I said it, GOSSIP about our own husband.

What is gossip? It is casual or unconstrained conversation or reports about other people typically involving details that are not confirmed as being true. (Source: Merriam Webster) And let's just be honest sister, at times you make up an entire lie in your head and assume things in your relationship and get mad at something that is not even true. Who knew you were the source of the own gossip in your head?

We complain about everything he does. We overthink every little thing he does and we talk about him to our friends. We do not go to our godly friends, either, we go find the "friend" who will agree with our dysfunction and complaining. We vent to her, not for godly advice, but to find someone to pat us on our backs and tell us how **GREAT** we are and how terrible our husband is. I do not know about you, but I want a friend that will say, "Heather, let's pray for your husband right now. Heather, I know it's hard right now, but the Lord is developing you and I believe Cornelius will get better because of your prayers and how you respond gently to Him."

In the midst of a test, you do not need some rebellious, loud mouthed woman telling you that your "man ain't nothin'" because sister, you thought he was something. **Otherwise, you wouldn't have married him.** At one point, you thought he was all of that. So, why do you bash your ex-whoever? The more you talk about him, after the fact, simply shows that your heart is still hurt and bitter. I sympathize with you and he may have hurt you very badly. I do not want to ignore that fact. But, I do want to encourage you to forgive whoever hurt you and let God heal your broken heart. Do not let yourself go spiritually and physically and totally give up on God and men. **If anything, invest MORE in Jesus.** Invest MORE in yourself. Work out, paint your nails, and do not just eat a bunch of ice cream and cookies. If you allow your emotions to overwhelm you, you will not only feel depressed, but you will start to gain weight and begin to feel worse about yourself.

Did you know that eating certain foods can actually depress you? I discussed this in my second book, "A Perfect Recipe." Food is supposed to energize you and give you more energy. Unfortunately, a lot of the food we eat does not do that. If anything, it weighs us down gives us what we call the "-itis." We feel heavy because we are mixing pastas and starches with animal proteins. So, it takes too much work for your digestive system to break down all of these foods. So what happens? You get sluggish and tired. The last thing you need in the midst of a test is to feel terrible physically. I believe that in addition to satan and his little demons attacking you, you can play a greater part in the way you feel physically.

Since we are discussing your physical look, I want to encourage you to find clothes that work for your body, work out, go on YouTube and learn how to do makeup and go thrifting! You may not think you need makeup or that you need to change your look, but stop what you doing and go look in the mirror. No, seriously. Did you do it? Ok, if it is late and you have PJ's on, that is fine, but really think about how you present yourself. And, I am going to say this, although I may get some emails about it, know that I am saying in this in the most loving matter: *Stop dressing like a man.* Put away your basketball shorts that you wear 24-7 and the huge t-shirts. No, seriously. If you are wearing Jordan's and sweats every single day, you may not attract the godly man you want in the suit and tie. Comb down that pony tail and pull yourself together sister! And honestly, you may not want a man in a suit and a tie, but your guy does not want to see you dressed down every single day! Communicate with him and maybe put on a sundress every now and then, some lipstick and perfume!

In discussing the physical, it is always so touchy because as Christians, we want to ignore at times this factor and say, "I'm saved! He needs to love me for me!" I get it sister, and I am sure he does. But, if you are married or seriously courting, ask him how he likes for you to dress. Most likely, you already know OR he is tired of arguing with you so he will say, *"Whatever you are comfortable in sweetheart."* But deep down, he may not feel comfortable sharing that he likes to see you in sundresses every now and then! It is sure not everything, but it can be something. So, look nice, smell good and be intentional daily about your physical appearance.

I recall when I went to this beauty store and I found clip on bangs while browsing. I was so excited! I wanted to change my look so I bought the bangs and I brought them home to surprise my husband. I knew that he did not like me in bangs, but I figured, "since they are clip-on bangs, I can clip them on and then I can clip them off. " So, I got home and clipped on the bangs and I showed my husband. His face dropped because I jokingly said, "Babe! I got a haircut, do you like it?!" And he was like, "No you didn't. I'm not crazy about them babe." So, I laughed and took them off and then one day we were headed out on a date night and I put the bangs on and I walked downstairs. He looked at me and said, "Babe, I like you better without the bangs." HUH? Babe. I mean. They're such a fun winter look, you don't like them?" as I walked to take them off. What good is it if I look good to everybody else but my husband does not like my hair? You see, I want to look good for my husband and my husband alone. If I am trying to please everybody else but him, *he is going to feel like it is all about me* pleasing others and not my spouse. You may think this mindset is crazy, but I am reminded of: Matthew 19:5 *"A man shall leave his father and his mother and hold fast to his wife, and the two shall become one flesh. They are no longer two, but one flesh"* (KJV).

Now, sister girl, you keeping those clip on bangs on your head shows you are two and not one. When you get married, you had better be prepared to die to yourself, that attitude and that idea of, "Ain't nobody going to tell me what to do." The TWO become ONE flesh. **You are one flesh.** When we get married we have to let who we used to be die for the BETTER. So, we need to put to death that rebellious, jezebel heart. We have to truly let God reveal to us why we act the way we do and why we would allow division to come into our marriage by some clip-on hair. I know that sounds silly, but it happens all the time. *If you are not ready to take off the bangs, you are not ready to get married.*

And, if you are single, you can ask yourself a question: **Am I ready to really remove my bangs?** My husband also prefers my hair brown versus platinum blonde. He met me as a blonde but he likes a darker look on me. He is ok with me getting highlights for the summer and here and there but I am sure to ask him prior to getting it done. So, single woman, what is your communication like with God? Do you ask Him for permission to wear certain things or how you should style your hair? Your heart must be so sensitive to His leadings that he should be telling you how to wear your hair and how you should dress. *Do you even ask Him?* We must practice obedience to Jesus whether single or married because we love God and we want to submit to Him. Then, if we DO get married, it sure makes submission much easier.

Now, back to hair. If you are married or you have a fiancé and you are considering going "natural" and cutting off all of your hair and he is totally opposed to it, *then why would you do it?* Oh, because of the health of your hair? **What about the health of your marriage?** Do you fight harder for a hairstyle or do you fight harder for your marriage? I actually know of a woman that cut off all of her hair after he husband was totally against it. She went ahead because she said "it is her hair and she can do what she wants to do." She simply showed her rebellious heart. She showed her lack of respect and honor for her husband's wishes. You may think that I am extreme, but it showed her heart as a woman and it showed why they are having the problems they are having in their marriage. *It is deeper than the hair.* You see, her rebellion stemmed long before she cut her hair. She has been in rebellion in her marriage for years and years. Cutting her hair was only proof of what was happening in her heart.

Understand that I am talking to you as the woman, I DO believe that men have a part to play in loving you like Christ loved the church and my husband wrote a great book on it called, "So, You Want to Be a Man?" But, this is the problem! We read these books and bitterness grows in our heart as we say, "WHAT about me?" Why am I doing all of the growing and changing? Why am I the one not cutting my hair? Why, why, why, why?

CHAPTER 8

Why Me?

I can answer your question from the last chapter. Do you often feel unappreciated? Ever felt like you are constantly pouring out, but the ones you love are not pouring back into you? Why you? Well, ask yourselves a couple of questions: What is your motive for doing what you do? Do you do what you because you absolutely love Jesus and you want to live for Him? Or, do you do what you do so because somebody will give you a cookie and tell you how wonderful you are?

For example, my husband's love language according to Gary Chapman's "The Five Love Languages" is "Acts of Service." So he feels most loved when I am cooking, cleaning and doing things for him, which totally is NOT fun. I would rather curl up and cuddle on the couch but, this man feels most loved when I am washing the dishes, which is not my area whatsoever. *It is funny how God pairs you with someone who really develops you and pushes you towards Him.* Nonetheless, one day I canceled my crazy, busy schedule and I cleaned the house for about six hours, cooked his favorite meal and he did not say anything or even attempt to love me back based on my touching love language. *As I sat there quietly, growing bitter in my heart,* the Lord asked me a question: "Heather, did you do what you did for a response from your husband or did you do it for me?

My response: "UMM, ME JESUS!! I wanted him to love me back based on my love language. I wanted him to tell me how great of a wife I was and cuddle with me for the rest of the day! How dare he not respond to my greatness?" Quite full of myself right, yeah, I agree. When we do things for ourselves expecting to be noticed we become bitter and weary. **When we do things for God He really strengthens us.** But, the problem is this: *We continue to do things in our own ability and our own way and set ourselves up for heartache for when we do not get the response we want from others. What happens then is our heart is hardened against that person and GOD.* When we harden our hearts against that friend, ex, husband or whoever, we are also hardening our hearts against Jesus.

Then, what happens? Because your heart is hardened against your man, your family, your boss, your co-worker or your friend you are now bothered and you do not feel like spending time with God because you know if you spend time with God He is going to check your funky attitude. He is going to soften your heart. He is going to show you where you are wrong and tell you, "YOU need to change." **Even** if the other person is in the wrong, He will show you how to lovingly respond and that he rewards you for loving people that are not being loving towards you.

But, you do not "feel like all that." You feel like being in your emotions. You feel like throwing a fit. *I just wonder how many answers to our problems are in the Bible, but we missed them because we did not read it that morning?* While you are having a fit, God is telling you that it is time to mature and grow up because for the last fifteen years you have said that you love Jesus but, you are still a nine month old spiritually. You have not grown past the milk of the word and you refuse to eat the meat of the word. **You like your tantrums.** You like your fits. All the while, it is satan's very attempt to get you to give up on your marriage, husband, single life, and family. All because of an emotional meltdown.

Satan reminds you to be like him, which is "selfish," asking, "what about ME?" Satan encourages you to have a pity party and then go and find a bunch of emotional women who will agree with your *crazy*. Then these professional wailers will all sit down and talk more about your emotions and how you are "so right." Instead, ask God to bring friends into your life who will be brutally honest with you. Who will totally check you and tell you, "Honey, you are being emotional. I love you, but you know you are in the wrong." I believe God WILL send some great accountably buddies your way throughout life and it is the Holy Spirit's job to show you who is the "real deal." Do not push away those real-deal friendships. Let them help you on your journey.

Well, sister, Jesus is calling you out. It is time to stop going around that same mountain over and over again. It is so easy to sing the song, "I surrender all Lord, I surrender all to You, take all of me." And then as soon as you leave church, get into the car, you pick your life back up and live exactly how you want to live it. Surrender? You surrender at church. But, after church, your life is your own. It is time for us to get serious about our walk with Him again. I know that even if you have been saved for years and are mature in your walk that sometimes, it just gets plain hard. I write this with tears in my eyes because at times, **I do not want to pray.** At times, I do not want to help people. At times, I want to be selfish. There is a constant war going on in my spirit to live for Jesus, free from the distractions of this world. I just want my heart to look like His. Therefore, I have to accept it is going to *cost me my entire life.*

Do you know what I love about God's sweet presence? He really shows me myself. He gives me a brand new perspective and in a moment, **my insecurities turn to boldness and trust in Him.** Then, He gently reminds me that if I am going to truly live for Jesus, I am going to have to take on some of his sufferings, including dying to my emotional self and shutting up. He begins to challenge my daily decisions.

Here's some ways that He challenged my daily activities. I did not think there was anything wrong with some of these things. I just thought that I was "strong" enough to handle the shows, the music, the whatever else until I started to see it seep into my heart, my attitudes, my words, my marriage and my life.

- This walk is going to cost you turning off the garbage on TV. I am not going to name any shows but, if it encourages fornication, adultery, anger or anything else that resembles the heart of satan, turn it off. Whether you believe it or not, a seed is being planted in your heart. That seed will grow up and harvest something. Not only that, the more attention you give to the TV, the less you will desire God. Did you not know that whatever you give your attention to is what you will desire? You do not desire God because you push His time and Word to the side because you may feel bored with it and turn on something that will entertain you. Television is "Telling-you-a-vision." What vision do you see for your life? Make sure that your shows are lining up with that vision.

- Your music. Now, you know I talked about this in *Pink Lips & Empty Hearts*. I am not trying to skip around here with a stick and tell you what to listen to on a regular basis, but if I can be totally real with you, Tupac used to be my favorite rapper as a young teenager. I knew all of his songs; albums and my life reflected it. I was angry. I was insecure. I was lonely. I watched pornography at the age of 15. But, when I gave my heart to Jesus in 2003, I remember sitting in my car outside of my apartment and trashing all of those CD's. The taste was kicked out of my mouth. It is like He took my blinders off and I began to see the truth. You see, when you get in Christ, He begins to take your bad desires away. *He takes them away and you will not return back to them a few weeks later.* When it is really Him, you have this encounter where you just do not want to sin anymore. You are pursuing HIM and not your sin. There is times in my own life where I know I should not be doing something so I ask God to help me to want to do the right thing and to stay on the righteous path. He works with a willing heart. And if you are married and you feel like you have to listen to "love songs" to get in the mood, ask yourself this question: *Why is my spouse not enough for me to get into the mood? Why do I need all of these outside things in order to get turned on by my spouse?* Why can I not trust God's presence to make our sex life beautiful in our marriage, free from secular music and distractions?

- You may have to let go of some of your "friends." Hanging out with a bunch of "what about me" women will cause you to eventually pick up that spirit. If you are going to be around that person, even if it is your sister, you have to make sure that you are not picking up what she is delivering to you.

You may say, "Heather, it does not take all that! Actually, it does take all that. When you truly give your life to Jesus, **there is a standard**. A standard that says, "You are not like this world. You cannot continue to think and act like this world. "So, it is going to cost you something. Are you willing to pay the price? Or, do you give up, make your own decisions while asking God, "Where ARE YOU?"

CHAPTER 9

Where are You, Lord?

Have you ever just felt like you are paying the cost of living for Jesus, but at times, it seems like it is so hard to spend time with God. Then, when you stop spending time with God, you begin to make assumptions about how He views you. You try to do all of this work to get Him to approve of you, but He has been right there all along, encouraging you and reminding you He wants your entire heart. I have definitely felt this way before, and I usually feel this way when my busy schedule replaces the time I spend with God and I seek after my goals instead of Him. I begin to make my own decisions, I stop acknowledging God and I acknowledge myself. Then, I get tired, worn out, weary and I start taking out my frustrations on the ones I love the most.

I like this example of a couple named Tim and Susan. They met and fell in love. They talked all of the time and soon became engaged. Once engaged, they started to argue all of the time and they were not as excited as they were when they first met. So, they finally get married and they stop communicating all together. Assumption and bitterness fester in their marriage and they start to grow apart. As they continued to argue, Susan would spend hours upon hours at work. The new transfer from another department was so nice to her! He would give her the attention she desired and complemented her. Susan began to rationalize in her heart, "I deserve this and if Tim wasn't arguing with me so much, I wouldn't have to run to work for attention." Soon, the emotional affair turned into a physical affair. Tim found out and they ended up divorced.

Sad story, right? I agree. **But sadly, this very story happens to you and your relationship with God.** You are excited when you first get saved. You are thrilled! You tell everyone about Jesus! You cry out to Him daily, He becomes your life. Then, when you really start to submit your life to Him, (engaged) it gets hard. Tests and trials come your way, but instead of facing them head on, you run from God. You run back to your past, back to what was once comfortable and into the arms of another person.

You run into the arms of your job and become a workaholic. Filling your God-voids with random online dating, online shopping and social media. You run into the arms of an ex-boyfriend that you know is not any good for you, but because you guys have a sex-understanding you continue to feed that relationship. You feel warm again. But, what you do not understand is that that man you are online dating is also dating ten other women. He is not totally focused on getting to know you because it is like speed dating to him. And hearing from the Lord? Psh, he is hearing from his flesh. And that man you keep sleeping with? He is sleeping with you and about five other women. *The woman he is about to sleep with tomorrow night will give him HIV/AIDS and he is about to pass it onto you in three days if you get back into the bed with him.* God is calling you back to Him and He is trying to warn you to stay away from that man but you think you are in too deep. But aren't in too deep.

The blood of Jesus cleanses you from all unrighteousness and you can stand boldly before God and ask for help in your time of need. (Hebrews 4:16-Paraphrase). Not only will God cleanse you, but He will free you from that messed up relationship and make you whole again. He will remind you of your worth and purpose. He will show you how so and so is not allowed in your heart anymore. You may say, "Heather, well, I'm not making an idol out of my job, I'm married and my bed is empty or with my spouse. These areas may not apply to you but you can insert your struggle here: _____. What is it? Porn?

Masturbation? Lying? Regardless of what you are struggling with, God wants you back.

Did you know that God even cares about the situations that you PUT yourself in? He has a plan to get you back on track and He wants you to stop ASSUMING He hates you. He wants you to stop running to this world for comfort. *He wants you to stop chasing after a bunch of people who do not care about you.* He wants you to stop leading your own life. Ask yourself this questions: Have I divorced God in my heart and gone my own way? Do I need to get back to a place of surrender? If so, do not wait for the music. Do not wait for church on Sunday. Do not wait for Bible study on Wednesday. Stop what you are doing and pour your heart out to Jesus. **Just let it out.** Cry, scream, kick, and tell God how mad you are. Tell Him how broken you feel. Tell Him you are jealous, bitter, hurt, and mad. You see, God can work with you when you are being honest because He already knows you! If you hate your husband and you are sick and tired of being sick and tired, then pour your heart out to God! Do you think God does not know who your husband is and can give you the insight on how to deal wisely with Him? And why are we holding bitterness and hurt against our spouse and relationships? Do not think that I am pointing fingers at you without also pointing them at myself. There are times when I want to throw my husband's past in his face, but then I ask myself a few questions:

1. Is it profitable?
2. Will it solve anything?
3. Will it start a huge argument?
4. Am I pursuing peace?
5. Am I building him up or tearing him down?

Then, I'm reminded of Matthew 6:15 "But if you refuse to forgive others, your Father will not forgive your sins."

If I can be totally honest, I am reminded of a huge argument that never took place last night. My husband had a lot on his mind and I felt like he was not completely paying attention to me when I was talking to him. Knowing he had a lot on his mind, I took a moment and I asked myself the above questions. And then, in retrospect I said to myself: "My husband is a good man. He is faithful, honest, loving, kind and is always there for our family. He is a wonderful father and how pointless is it for me to focus on the little he does not do in comparison to what he DOES do as the man of this house." So, instead of bashing him, I am going to focus on what he does as an awesome husband and father. Then, I take my issue to God because I believe He solves issues much better than I can solve them. After I take it to

God, I really leave it there. So, as I went through this process in my mind, my husband began to open up to me and share his heart. We were able to go to bed in peace because I did not overreact and complain about him not paying attention to me and he was able to get some things off of his chest as well. "Well, Heather, what about you?" Me? We are one flesh. My focus is pleasing my body and my husband is one with me. Heather Canter died when she took on the name of Heather Lindsey. What if I would have given it to God but picked it back up again and started a fight?

Far too often, we take our issues to God, *but we pick them back up again*, meditate on them and then we push them underneath the rug. Then, our struggles and problems seep through the rug into our relationships six months down the line, a year down the line, or even ten years down the line. You have to be intentional about casting down those crazy thoughts and making them submit to God's word! (Paraphrased from 2 Corinthians 10:5)

Do you want to know where God is? He is exactly where you left Him when you leaned on bitterness, your job, that man or whatever else. I believe at some times we deliberately violate our conscience.

First Timothy 1:19 tells us this: "Cling to your faith in Christ, and keep your conscience clear. For some people have deliberately violated their consciences; as a result, their faith has been shipwrecked."

This verse describes something we do to ourselves. We should ask ourselves from time to time: How do we deliberately violate our conscience?

1. When we openly reject God's leadings
2. When we know what to do but we refuse to do it.

Let's bring it just a little closer to home with a few examples:

1. When you keep little Johnny, Tommy and Billy Joe in your bed when God told you that he was not the one.
2. When you openly rebel against your husband and ignore his headship.
3. When you cuss somebody out instead of shutting up and letting God fight your battles
4. When you gossip about your friends.
5. When you watch garbage on TV.
6. When you listen to garbage music.

You see, when Timothy wrote that scripture, he was totally inspired by God. God knew that if you were to do those things, it would plant seeds in your heart. **Those seeds will grow up and have the potential to ruin your life.** Those seeds will grow up and make you doubt God. Those seeds will grow up and make you feel like God is not real. Those seeds will grow up and potentially turn into massive rotten trees called divorce. People do not "all the sudden" get a divorce. A divorce happens day-by-day, moment-by-moment. It happens in one small argument here and another disagreement there. One disrespectful comment, one day of ignoring your spouse and refusing to change. We have to STOP giving satan an open door into our relationships. Some of us scream, "devil, I bind you. Get away from my marriage," and then turn right around and start an argument with our spouses.

I challenge you beautiful crown, to do your part. Guard your heart. If you are close to God you will know He is always there and He will never leave you or forsake you. You will know that even when times get rough you do not depend on your feelings but on His word.

CHAPTER 10

The Money Struggle

This area is such a huge struggle for women. They have this idea that their husband is supposed to be the "Provider" so they look to their husband to provide all of their needs. For example, if you meet a good man who loves Jesus, you have peace about him, he has vision, knows his purpose, has a job, is faithful to his job, but is not making the amount of money you would like, so you pass on him because he is not making the "six figures." The problem is this, we have a bunch of women who get saved but *they don't renew their minds*. Money is not everything, honey. You can have a huge rock on your finger with a million dollars in the bank and the house can be EMPTY on love. Stop chasing paper, Christian woman, and chase Christ. There is something about building your kingdom together with your guy focusing on Christ and not money. If money and that temporary comfort is your focus, you will look up, be eighty years old and still be single.

The thing is this, if we look at the word "Provider" it is supposed to be for your NEEDS. Not the selfish, foolish things you want. If I can be totally real with you, if you do not believe in your husband or boyfriend, *then no money in the world will change your heart.* **Prior to the ring, you have to believe in him.**

My husband worked at a mega-church for four years and we met while he was working there as the chief of staff. He was one of the youngest executives on staff. He had a house, a car, a stable job, benefits and all of the perks of working for a church. You know, the front seat at church, his own parking spot and whatever else. Not that those things mattered, but it sure was nice to show up late at church and know that you always have a parking spot and a seat. Three months after we got married, the Lord told my husband to quit his job and to move to Jackson, Mississippi to study and read his bible. Most women would think, "Ummm, why can't you do that in Atlanta while you work a full time job?" or "How are we going to eat because praying doesn't pay the bills." Thankfully, I was working a full time job at a software hedge accounting firm, as I mentioned earlier, in the human resources department. I worked from home so I was able to take my job with me to Jackson. And because we are married, our finances become ONE. God used my job to help provide for our family so my husband could prepare for ministry. If I could be totally honest, if any other man said that they are about to quit their high paying job to go pray in another state, I would call him crazy. But, I believe in my husband and I believed in him then. If he said that we are going to move to Alaska, I would be online researching a snowsuit and packing my bags. I honor, respect, submit to and support my husband. So, what about you? Are you hindering what God called your family to do because you are nagging your head and trying to stop what God called your family to do? I believe that there are many women that are challenging what God called their husbands to do. It is TIME for you to move out of the way so *your guy can properly lead you.* Now, this life is not about chasing paper sisters. God truly provided for our family then and he continues to provide for us. We definitely had our share of eating vegetables for dinner, but we simply trusted God. I did not call my girlfriends and call my man "sorry" because he was not working. *I prayed for my husband daily and proclaimed that he heard God's voice and a voice of a stranger he did not follow (John 10:4-5).* I prayed for God to lead him as he submitted his life to Jesus. **I listened to my husband's ideas and encouraged him where God led me.** I spoke up when I felt like certain business ideas were going in a wrong direction.

While my husband was in this season of not working and just studying and praying, I did have a moment. My moment was this: "God! Why can't you open the right door for him? I could pay down some of our debt much faster if we were both working!" **Then, God reminded me that my paycheck was our paycheck.** And if I continue to think that the money is mine, He will humble me while reminding me once again how my pride would not get me very far and that I must place my hope in Jesus.

I recall one of Cornelius's old acquaintances was investing in this stock and he was getting all of these people to invest. He asked Cornelius to invest in the stock and Cornelius asked me for my opinion. I told him that I had no peace about it and I am 100% against him investing. Thankfully, my husband listened to me because down the line we found out that the investor was stealing everyone's money and it was a Ponzi scheme. My husband and I talk about everything and I thank God he trusts me. Thank God that he really listens to me when I speak up. I truly believe it is because I do not always speak up about **every little issue**. Some things are best left unsaid and we need to *learn the spirit of "shut up."* Before you get mad at me, the spirit of "patience" is a fruit of the spirit. We have to be patient at times and let God speak to our husbands. I speak up when I really believe my husband is going the wrong way and thankfully, it is not often. Even if your husband seems to make bad decisions all of the time, take his sins and weaknesses to God. It is God alone who truly changes a man's heart. Your nagging won't change anything.

So, if you are single, check out that man's submission to the Lord. You will need to see some proof in his pudding before you get married. If you do not believe in him, trust him, respect him, or honor him, you will constantly undermine him in the marriage. If you are married, ask God to help you to respect him again as your head. Even if he messed up really bad in your marriage, God honors submission, even if you do not think he earned it or deserves it. Sometimes, we think we can put a price tag on believing in our spouse, like *"he has to earn my respect, he has to earn my this or that—especially after he messed up."* **What if Jesus did that in regards to forgiving you when you messed up?** If we consider it in this way, it immediately humbles us. It reminds us that we are not perfect and we are in need of our Savior daily. It reminds us how bickering and fighting about money is meaningless. It reminds us that it is all Gods money anyway.

Psalm 24:1 *"Tells us that the earth is the LORD's, and everything in it. The world and all its people belong to Him."* So, search your heart. Who is your true provider? Is it your job? Is it your savings account?

I have learned that when you place your entire hope in your savings as you claim to place your hope in Jesus, you may get tested to prove to you how your heart really does not belong to Him. I know this may sound harsh, but the reality is we have all placed our trust in someone or something temporary.

I recall when I left my full time job to go into ministry and I had a really nice savings account stocked up to cover our bills for about 6 months. Then, my transmission went out on my car, the key stopped working and then a few other major issues with my truck. And guess when this happened? On the last day of my job and I was invoiced for a few thousand dollars by the dealership! I was shocked! As I paid the amount, the Lord reminded me I was placing too much trust in my savings. He reminded me He provides for my family and I need to not place my trust in a piece of paper.

So, I ask you this question successful sister: are you making your "future hubby list" and checking it twice, making sure it has that he makes a certain amount of money? You will learn very quickly money can never change your struggles. You can live in a million dollar house and be totally empty on love, while your husband is spending your families' money on strippers. You want to marry a man who first and foremost totally and completely loves Jesus. If he is pure in heart and has a vision, purpose and is sensitive to the Lord's leading, *then you cannot put a price tag on that comfort.* I know you want to, I know you want to be comfortable financially but I am reminded of Luke 16:13. Luke says, "*No one can serve two masters. For you will hate one and love the other; you will be devoted to one and despise the other. You cannot serve both God and money.*"

So, do yourself a favor, right now, and ask what is in your heart? Ask God if you really want HIS best for your life, or do you want society's best for your life? I once dated guys that made millions of dollars and then I took a moment to actually look at them. I looked into their eyes and just saw darkness. These guys had made money their god. And because money was their god, they lived by money's godless standards. They were led by money and their focus was to obtain more money. The whole "honor your one-day marriage, spouse, love Jesus with your whole heart, mind, soul and strength" was totally out of the door because they felt like, "why do I need God? I have everything." So, they thought. On one occasion, after really looking into his heart, I asked him, "What do you think about a relationship with Jesus?" He said, "You know, I've been saved my whole life and I was in the church when I was little. I don't go now, but God knows my heart." Huh? Ok, so you do not live for Jesus;

you do not talk like He did; you do not spend time with Him; you do not attend service; you have no accountability; you think its ok to have sex with me, curse everybody out, lie to me—*because I know you have many chicks on the side, I checked your cell phone.* So, you think that you are saved? No, sir. You are not saved. And I am not the one judging you." I just read 1 John 2:3-6:

> *"We know that we have come to know him if we keep his commands. Whoever says, 'I know him,' but does not do what he commands is a liar, and the truth is not in that person. But if anyone obeys his word, love for God is truly made complete in them. This is how we know we are in him: Whoever claims to live in him must live as Jesus did."*

As I continued to examine my relationship with him, I looked at his face. **Wait, I'm not totally attracted to you.** How did pieces of paper from a tree blind me to the fact I would not date you if you were broke? Wait, and the fact you flirt with other women and I keep finding inappropriate messages in your phone number? I may only be nineteen years old, but I can read sir and your **heart is clearly with so many.** Oh, and his personality? Well, he is cool. But a cool personality will not sustain an entire marriage and lead my future family in the way that it is supposed to go. Did I really let my standards slide for this man? My prayer is that the couple men I did dated when I was single give their hearts to Jesus. I truly wish nothing but the best for all of them.

I want you to know that your hope can never be in money or finances. I have learned over time finances are one of the number one reasons for divorce. So, be sold on the foundation of a man, which should be Christ and not his bank account.

Ask God if your deal breakers come from HIM or you. At times, we can say we really love Jesus and our heart is committed to Him, but we compare our lives to other women and their husbands. I recall talking to a woman on the phone one day. She shared with me she married her husband because they have kids together and a history. It also did help that he was a multi-millionaire. But now, she looks back over everything that has happened and realized money does not mean everything and just because you have a child with a person does not mean you should get married to them. One day, you will either, look up in regret and wish you would have obeyed God, or, you will look up with great joy because you trusted God.

I want you to know that even the godliest marriages have their struggles. As you may read in my first book, Pink

Lips and Empty Hearts, my husband and I waited to kiss until our wedding day. You would think that waiting to kiss meant we really had it all together after the "I do." Psh, please! That is when the REAL work started. Waiting those little twenty months was nothing compared to the giant in our marriage called **selfishness.** I had a lot of crap in my heart from the past. My husband had a lot of hurt from his past. And now, you have two people with hurts and past memories coming together and becoming one flesh! It was plain HARD those first couple years! We still have to work on our marriage DAILY but we flow together much better now than we did the first year. So, with all of that being said, I am thankful to be "soul tied" to my husband.

We always talk about soul ties as being a bad thing, but what about when you marry God's best, then it becomes a powerful soul tie that brings God glory! This is why you cannot afford to be unequally yoked with an unbeliever. You are going to be yoked and tied to his past, to his god, to his mindset, to his ways. And honey, the scripture does not change just because he is not saved. We still GET to submit onto our husband as ONTO the Lord (Ephesians 5:22). You may say, "I don't have to submit to him because he isn't saved!" Well, is he asking you to do anything illegal or anything you would not do as onto the Lord? Then, do not do it. But, for most of you he is telling you not to go somewhere. Or, maybe to spend more time with the kids. Or, something else along those lines—nothing illegal. So, how do you expect to win him over (*1 peter 3:1 says, "In the same way, you wives must accept the authority of your husbands. Then, even if some refuse to obey the Good News, your godly lives will speak to them without any words. They will be won over to Jesus by your 'quiet and gentle' spirit.*) if you are rebellious, loud and you ignore him? He does not feel respected or honored by you because you throw the Bible at him as if it is you and God against your husband. I am sure you belittling him will not make Him want to run to Jesus. So, way before the ring, let us do our part. Let us make sure our deal breakers are coming from Jesus, and not our old self. And, if we are married to an unbeliever, let us just continue to believe the best.

A Father's Love

I say all of this to say that God loves you and has a plan for your life. One day, when you leave this earth there will be footprints down the hallway coming to get you, to take you to a destination for eternity. Will those footsteps be satan's demons, taking you to hell or will angels be singing and worshiping God as they rejoice that He has made another His own. Most of the things I mentioned in this book come FAR after your heart is SET on and ESTABLISHED in Jesus Christ. Most of the physical things mean nothing in comparison to Jesus Christ and eternity. However, God placed it heavy on my heart to address a few of these simple areas that seem to get overlooked and may be effecting your outlook on life. Living for Jesus will take your entire life and your body is the temple where the Holy Spirit resides. In order to have the time and the energy to do what God called us to do, we must be disciplined in our eating, in working out and in taking care of our bodies.

As a mother, I want to see Logan accomplish the will of God for his life and do what the Lord tells him to do. I want to see him healthy, strong and focused—inside out. As a parent, it is hard to discipline Logan. I started sleep training Logan when he was about seven months. As a breastfeeding mom, I learned that if I allow Logan to sleep in my bed, he will nurse all night long because he can smell my breast milk. It is like placing a plate a "fresh out of the oven" chocolate cookies next your bed. You can wake up and get a quick snack and go back to sleep. Well, I was one tired chocolate chip cookie! It was time for me to start sleep training! Was it hard for Logan? Absolutely! When I first started, he screamed and screamed and screamed and since I do not believe in the "cry out" method, I would go into his room every 10 minutes to soothe him and let him know I was right there and that I never left him. I would remind him that he is loved and I care. Over time, the tests and trails developed him into a little boy who actually slept through the night and could physically put himself to sleep without our help! As a good parent, I cannot just let Logan sleep in our bed for the rest of his life. At some point, he has to learn to fall asleep by himself. And, so do you. At some point you have to go from the milk of the word to the meat of the word.

First Corinthians 3:1-3 (KJV) says "And I, brethren, could not speak unto you as unto spiritual, but as unto carnal, even as unto babes in Christ. I have fed you with milk, and not with meat: for hitherto ye were not able to bear it, neither yet now are ye able. For ye are yet carnal: for whereas there is among you envying, and strife, and divisions, are ye not carnal, and walk as men?"

So, no more meaningless arguments and silly strife. Instead, start to spend time with Jesus. He longs for your attention. I love to share stories of my son because they remind me of the Father's love for us. A few weeks ago, I went away for a couple days on a speaking engagement. The entire time, I face timed and called Logan. Although at times he did not totally pay attention to me while I was on the phone, I longed for his attention. As soon as I rushed home, I grabbed Logan and I started to nurse him! I missed the closeness we shared and I longed for it all weekend! *I wonder if God is the same way with us?* If He loves us more than an earthly parent can love their child, I'm sure He misses us in a way I would never understand. God misses you. Yes, you. He misses being intimate with you. When He calls you and reaches out to you—you seem so distracted. He longs for quiet, one-on-one time with you, to be one with you again.

At some point, we have to grow up in this walk so we can in turn, help others out of their pit. So, do your part on this earth. Wake up every morning and spend time with God and give Him a chance to fill you up again. So many of us are so focused and rushing around for our goals we forget God. We no longer have time to sit at his feet and study the word and we do not think he talks fast enough for us, so we run to social media and preachers for life's answers. There is nothing more precious than you sitting at the feet of Jesus and letting Him change you! How do you do that?

Wake up every morning, turn on worship music, pray, walk around, dance, and get your mind set on Him. Then, pull out your journal and write down whatever God places on your heart. This is a safe place to vent your hurts and pains. Grab a bible and read it as God leads you. If you do not know what to study, simply study an area you are struggling with (i.e., Fear, worry, etc.) and talk to God. Pray, vent and then apply what you learned throughout your day. So, are you too busy? Too tired? At some point, we have to stop with the excuses and start finding a solution, and that solution is Jesus Christ. So, dust off your crown and get prepared to go through some things on this earth, even with every attempt to spend time with God. You will get distracted; end up tired, weary or feel like you cannot hear His voice.

Remember this: The crown that is waiting for you in heaven is a beautiful, vibrant crown. Everything you went through on this earth will be worth the crown awaiting you